Friends
Forever

D0005397

Other Titles by Marci
Published by
Blue Mountain Arts®

A Grateful Path
Inspirational Thoughts on Unconditional Love,
Acceptance, and Positive Living

To My Mother
Your Love Is a Lasting Treasure

A Sister Always… A Friend Forever
A Celebration of the Love, Support, and Friendship Sisters Share

Library of Congress Control Number: 2007923652
ISBN: 978-1-59842-248-1

Children of the Inner Light is a registered trademark. Used under license.

◼ and Blue Mountain Press are registered in U.S. Patent and Trademark Office. Certain trademarks are used under license.

Printed in China.
First printing: 2007

✪ This book is printed on recycled paper.

This book is printed on fine quality, laid embossed, 80 lb. paper. This paper has been specially produced to be acid free (neutral pH) and contains no groundwood or unbleached pulp. It conforms with all the requirements of the American National Standards Institute, Inc., so as to ensure that this book will last and be enjoyed by future generations.

Blue Mountain Arts, Inc.
P.O. Box 4549, Boulder, Colorado 80306

8/26/09

Happy Birthday!

Carolyn.

Thank you for being

my friend! Love Toni

Friends
Forever

A Celebration
of Friendship and
Everything Friends Share
Through the Years

Marci

Blue Mountain Press™
Boulder, Colorado

Introduction

Friendship is one of our most valuable gifts. It completes our desire to love and be loved... to understand and be understood. It is that closeness that makes us feel connected... that brings fulfillment... and that lets us know that we are not alone in this world.

Friendship fills these universal needs, and at the same time, it gives us a glimpse of our own true nature. The exchanges of the heart that occur between friends create memories that last a lifetime, and those memories become treasures that warm us on the coldest of days.

Through the sharing of my writing, I have learned how much alike we are. We all want the same simple thing, which is to tell our loved ones that they "are truly loved." It is with great pleasure that I share my words with you. I hope they will give voice to your deepest feelings.

May your friendships bring you the joy of an everlasting bond.

Marci

I Am Grateful
for Our Friendship

As I travel my journey through life, I try to remember to be grateful for the things that really matter. I want you to know that one of the greatest blessings in my life is my friendship with you. You are the person I call when I need to talk, and I know that you will be there sometimes to "just listen." You are the person that I can laugh with about the most important life events. You "know me," and that saves words sometimes... Thank you for sharing your friendship with me.

Your Kind and Generous Spirit Shines Brightly in My Life

That's you!

Some people have a way of brightening someone's day... and it's with the little things that mean so much. There is a phone call at just the right time, a hug when it is needed, or a comforting word of encouragement. For me, that special person is you!

Time Spent with Friends
Creates Lifelong
Sweet Memories

Every time we're together, precious moments come flooding back, and I am reminded of all our laughter and joy through the years. I am so appreciative of those times and for having met you. Through the pain and sorrow, happiness and joy, we have learned much. Yours is the humor I can always count on and the friendship I know will last forever.

Our Lives Were Brought Together for a Reason

You are always ready to share
with me your experience, strength,
and hope, and when I need your
guidance, you offer me your
wisdom and your understanding.
You are there through the good
times and a constant light through
the bad. I know we were meant
to always be friends. Our bond
is everlasting!

Words Can't Describe
How Much
You Mean to Me

For all of the times you have come through for me... for all of the times you have listened instead of telling me what to do... for all of the times you have hugged away my troubles... for the laughs over nothing... for the many tears dried... you are a cherished friend!

Our Friendship
Was Meant to Be

I can't remember a time before
we were friends... it seems like
you have always been a part of my
life. When we first met, there was
that instant connection, and since
then our friendship has grown into
something that has brought me
so much joy. I am grateful for all
that you are... our friendship was
"meant to be."

You always understand what is in my heart. You are there whenever I need you, listening and offering your insights. You look deeply enough to really see me, allowing me to understand the true meaning of friendship.

You listen and that lets me hear my own thoughts. Your insights help guide me toward solutions. You are never too busy when I need you, and that means so much to me. We have learned from each other. You are a blessing every day!

I Am Proud
to Call You My Friend

Always!

You handle life's ups and downs with grace and even remember to encourage others along the way. You face challenges with courage, compassion, and conviction. I am proud to call you my friend.

If I Had My Way...

All the good things you have brought to my life would be returned to you.

A guardian angel would always watch over you and whisper life's secrets in your ear.

★

Your steps would be guided through all of life's challenges, and your heart would remember its true calling.

Hope would be a constant light in your life, and love would warm your heart every day.

Your days would be filled with all the things that bring you lasting happiness.

There would be nothing but love and acceptance in your future.

When I look at you, I see
your kind and loving spirit.

When I think about the things that are important to me, I always think of you.

Your Friendship Is
a Constant Light…
Sometimes Lighting My Path,
Always Brightening My Day

When I want to talk… you listen. When I am down… you encourage me. When I am happy… you share my joy. When I am sad… your hug tells me that everything will be okay. You know my deepest hopes and my greatest dreams… you are everything I could ever want in a friend.

Thank You for...

...Your thoughtfulness, your caring, and your ability to give me hope in every situation.

...All that is uniquely you!

...Being a special light in my life.

...Being there through the years and always being my friend.

Friendship Is One of
Life's Greatest Treasures

Through the gift of friendship, we are given the opportunity to give and receive love while traveling the journey of life. We learn about "our best selves" as we meet the challenges to listen, to give support, and to be there when we are needed. Through the gift of friendship, we are reminded that some things do last forever, and friendship is one of them.

Friends Can Do
Anything or
Nothing and Have
the Best Time

And we do a lot of nothing, sometimes!

No matter how much time has passed between our visits, when we speak, we pick up right where we left off, and I am left with a feeling of happiness and excitement that is difficult to define. Thank you for coming into my life and sharing your special spirit with me.

Your Friendship Is like an
Angel's Wing,
Lifting Me Up at
Just the Right Time

You are always there... to help me fix the bad things, appreciate the little things, and remind me that the most important things in life are free! Your encouraging words and your faith in me are gifts beyond measure.

May You Be Blessed with
These Things That Last...
Faith, Hope, Love,
Family, and Friends

If you have faith, hope, love, family, and friends, whatever challenges life brings, you will get through. Your faith will light your path... hope will keep you strong... the love you give to others will bring you joy... and family and friends will bring you comfort.

As we travel our journeys, we find new friends, lose old friends, and often discover who our real friends are. We learn about love, reassess our lives, and often reevaluate our needs and our faith.

I have watched you change through the years, claiming "who you are" in your search for the true meaning of life. You should know that through it all, there is one thing that has not changed, and that is my friendship with you.

I'm So Glad We Have Each Other

When I think of you, I think, "What could be better than having someone to talk to who already knows all about me and loves me as I am?"

When I think of you, I think, "What could be more fun than sharing my joys with someone who is truly happy for me?"

When I think of you, I think, "What could be better than a friendship that has created so many wonderful memories?"

When I think of you, I think, "We're friends!" and I realize how lucky I am to have you!

I Know I Can Always
Depend on You

Some days we just need a hand to hold... Some days we just need a hug... Some days we just need a word of encouragement... Some days we just need someone to be there for a laugh and a memory... On my "some days," there is you! *Lucky me!*

♥

A friend's love is a gift that you unwrap a little bit each year.

A friend is the one you call when you need to talk to someone who knows your heart.

A friend walks beside you to share each day... stands beside you when you question yourself... and walks in front of you when you've lost your way.

A friend sees your beautiful spirit shining through on good days and bad.

I'm so glad you are my friend!

If I Searched the World,
I Could Never Find
a Better Friend

Carolyn

You are a perfect example of love and caring, compassion and concern. Just talking to you can make me feel better. Knowing that I have a friend like you is truly wonderful.

These Things I Wish for You

I wish you a life filled with love… a true love to share your every dream… family love to warm your heart… and priceless love found in the gift of friendship.

I wish you peace… peace in knowing who you are… peace in knowing what you believe in… and peace in the understanding of what is important in life.

I wish you joy... joy as you awaken each day with gratitude in your heart for new beginnings... joy when you surrender to the beauty of a flower or a baby's smile... and joy, a hundred times returned, for each time you've brought happiness to another's heart.

Good Friends
like You Are a Gift

Our relationship has added so much to my life, teaching me what it means to share honestly and reflect on my innermost feelings. You have shared your journey and helped me through mine. When I think of you, I realize if we have good friends, we have almost everything.

I Treasure
Your Presence
in My Life

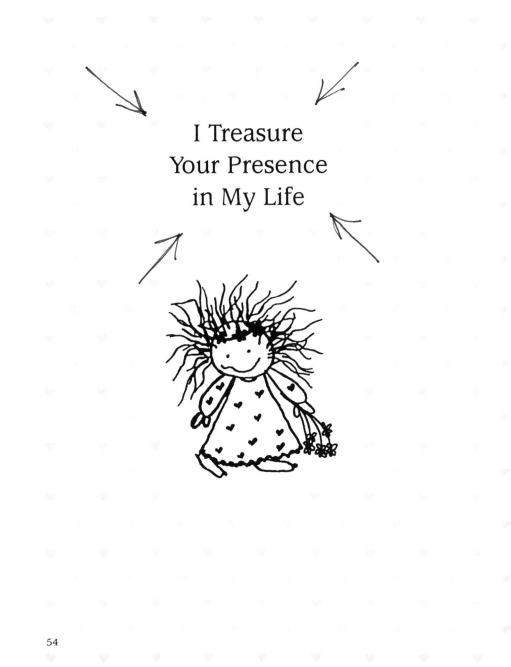

I have watched you cultivate your unique talents and have been inspired to do the same. I have watched you live with integrity, and this example has led the way. I have accepted the challenge to be my best self, as your encouraging words lifted me up. Watching you handle the ups and downs of life, and seeing you move always to higher ground, gives me a vision of my future.

Your Friendship
Has Made
Such a Difference
in My Life

There are people who change our lives, often without even realizing the impact they have made just by being themselves. You have made such a difference in my life. I am grateful for the way you are always willing to share the precious gift of time... for always believing in the best in people... for always seeing the bright side of things... for the many kind words you have spoken... for the thoughtful things you have done... The world needs more people like you!

You Are like Family to Me

You have taught me that what makes a "family" is not found in a name, it is found in the heart. You are so much more to me than a friend... you are like family. You listen to my dreams and remind me to believe in them. You are a part of every joy that comes my way, and I am so happy to have you in my life.

You Make Everything in My Life Better

You are there with love, encouragement, or a hug, and somehow you always seem to know just what I need. When I am down, you lift me up, forgiving my mistakes and helping me to forget them, too... When I need encouragement, you let me know that I am not alone... When I need a hug, you wrap your arms around me and tell me everything will be okay... When there are good times, we laugh and they are so much better... and when we share sorrow, it seems half as bad. I am glad that you are my special friend.

Simple Things
to Remember

Love is why we are here.

The most important day is today.

If you always do your best,
you will not have regrets.

Your enthusiasm for life and your
will to succeed will take you far.

When you need a hug I will
always be there with open arms.

Miracles happen every day
because angels are everywhere.

True friends see the best in you
and support you through challenges.

For all of your accomplishments,
nothing will bring you more happiness
than love and friendship.

No Matter How Busy Life Gets, You Are Always in My Heart

In today's world, life gets so busy that the days roll by and we realize we have not spoken to the ones we love! I want you to know that you are always in my heart... You are one of the most important people in my life, and even if we do not speak every day, my best thoughts and love are always with you.

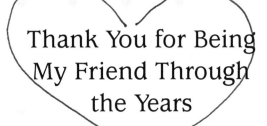

Thank You for Being
My Friend Through
the Years

I look back at everything we've shared and give thanks for our lasting friendship. We have shared joys and sorrows, and each "exchange of the heart" has made our friendship stronger. Together we have learned what it means to stand the test of time, and this lesson is invaluable.

Friends
Forever

Each time I see you, I am reminded of how special our friendship is. We have that special connection that comes along once in a lifetime. We have shared so much through the years... our hopes, our dreams, our joys, and our struggles. Thank you for being a part of my life and for always being my friend.

About Marci

Marci began her career by hand-painting floral designs on clothing. No one was more surprised than she was when one day, in a single burst of inspiration and a completely new and different art style, her delightful characters sprang from her pen! "Their wild and crazy hair is a sign of strength," she thought, "and their crooked little smiles are endearing." She quickly identified the charming characters as Mother, Daughter, Sister, Father, Son, Friend, and so on, until all the people and places in life were filled. Then, with her own loved ones in mind, she wrote a true and special sentiment to each one. This would be the beginning of a wonderful success story, which today still finds Marci writing each and every one of her verses in this same personal way.

Marci is a self-taught artist who has always enjoyed writing and art. She grew up working in her family's small grocery and sub shop. It was there, as she watched her dad interact with customers, she learned that relationships in the workplace and community, as well as in the family, provide the greatest satisfaction and joy.

She went on to develop a business from her home, making home-baked breads, cakes, and pastries to be sold in her dad's store. Later, she started another small home-based business hand-painting clothing for women. At first, she didn't have any idea she could paint and was amazed at how many people loved her work! She was gratified that she could create "wearables" that brought so much joy to those who wore them.

Now as she looks back, Marci sees how all her interests were pieces of a puzzle that fit together and gave her the skills she needed for her work today as artist and author. She is thrilled to see how her delightful characters and universal messages of love have touched the hearts and lives of people everywhere.